SERENA
WILLIAMS

BY ALEX MONNIG

SportsZone

An Imprint of Abdo Publishing
abdopublishing.com

abdopublishing.com

Published by Abdo Publishing, a division of ABDO, PO Box 398166, Minneapolis, Minnesota 55439. Copyright © 2018 by Abdo Consulting Group, Inc. International copyrights reserved in all countries. No part of this book may be reproduced in any form without written permission from the publisher. SportsZone™ is a trademark and logo of Abdo Publishing.

Printed in the United States of America, North Mankato, Minnesota
052017
092017

THIS BOOK CONTAINS
RECYCLED MATERIALS

Editor: Todd Kortemeier
Series Designer: Craig Hinton

Publisher's Cataloging-in-Publication Data

Names: Monnig, Alex, author.
Title: Serena Williams : tennis legend / by Alex Monnig.
Other titles: Tennis legend
Description: Minneapolis, MN : Abdo Publishing, 2018. | Series: Playmakers |
      Includes bibliographical references and index.
Identifiers: LCCN 2017930233 | ISBN 9781532111525 (lib. bdg.) |
      ISBN 9781680789379 (ebook)
Subjects: LCSH: Williams, Serena, 1981- --Juvenile literature. | Tennis player --
      United States--Biography--Juvenile literature.
Classification: DDC 796.342 [B]--dc23
LC record available at http://lccn.loc.gov/2017930233

TABLE OF CONTENTS

Serena Williams

CHAPTER 1

BUILDING A CHAMPION

Serena Williams stood at the baseline. The 17-year-old was one point away from her first Grand Slam title. Martina Hingis waited for Williams to serve. Hingis was the top seed in the 1999 US Open.

Williams prepared to start the point. She rocked back. She tossed the ball up with her left arm. Then she smashed it across the net. The white beads in her braids bounced on the back of her head.

Serena Williams celebrates a win at the 1999 US Open.

Hingis lunged to her right and swatted the ball back. The two players each hit a backhand. Williams hit another one. So did Hingis. But the ball floated high. Williams waited at the baseline. She was ready. But the ball sailed out of bounds. Williams could hardly believe it. She had beaten the top-ranked player in the world. She had won her first Grand Slam title.

> Any Grand Slam championship is memorable. But Serena Williams's 1999 US Open win carried even more meaning. It made her the first black woman to win the US Open since Althea Gibson did so in 1957 and 1958.

Williams screamed and cried. She went over to the stands to kiss her mother. The win was a dream come true. When she and her older sister Venus were growing up, they talked about which Grand Slam event they wanted to win the most. Serena always said the US Open.

The Williams sisters were destined to be tennis superstars. Serena was born in Saginaw, Michigan, on September 26, 1981.

Richard Williams and his daughters pose near a Compton tennis court in 1991.

Her family moved to Compton, California, when she was a baby. Compton was dangerous. There was gang violence and racism.

Serena's father, Richard, grew up in Shreveport, Louisiana. He and other black people were treated unfairly because of

Serena, *right*, and sister Venus Williams just days before Venus turned pro in 1994

their race. He did not want the same for Serena and Venus. So he introduced them to tennis. He hoped it would help them escape Compton.

Richard trained his daughters hard. They practiced for two hours a day. Serena was three years old when she started. Day after day, the sisters headed out into the Compton sun. The practice courts were in terrible shape. The ground was cracked. Weeds grew through the playing surface. Sometimes the courts did not even have nets.

Richard Williams tried to prepare his daughters for anything. He had other kids visit practice and yell mean things at Venus and Serena. He thought it would prepare the sisters to play in front of an angry crowd.

It was there that Serena learned how to play. Richard pushed his daughters to become great. Then he pushed them to become even better.

Serena Williams

CHAPTER 2

BECOMING ONE OF THE GREATS

It was time for Serena and Venus Williams to take the next step. In 1990 Richard Williams decided his daughters needed better training. So the family moved to Florida. Serena was nine. Richard wanted pro coach Rick Macci to work with them. The girls had power. But their form needed work. Macci helped them perfect their skills. One thing the girls did not lack was desire.

Sixteen-year-old Serena competes against Lindsay Davenport at the 1997 Ameritech Cup.

The coach noticed their play improved even more when they started competing.

Rick Macci is one of the best-known tennis coaches in the United States. He helped the Williams sisters become stars. He coached other tennis greats, too. Macci mentored Andy Roddick and Jennifer Capriati. They both won Grand Slam titles.

Serena started dominating the United States Tennis Association junior tour. She was the top-ranked player under age 10. Most players play hundreds of junior matches before turning pro. But Richard did not want his daughters playing too much. He wanted them to concentrate on school. There was a chance tennis wouldn't work out. So he wanted them to have an education too.

He also taught Serena and Venus about the value of helping others. The two young tennis stars made appearances

Serena returns a shot at the 1998 Australian Open, her first Grand Slam event.

for various charities. They later started their own foundation.
On the court, it was time for Serena to take the next step. Venus had already made her pro debut on October 31, 1994. Almost exactly one year later, Serena made hers. On October 28, 1995, she played her first pro tennis match.

As Serena's popularity has grown, so has her charity work. She has donated time and money to several causes. She has helped pay for new schools in Africa. She has also donated to help families that have been affected by gun violence. The Serena Williams Fund helps pay for students to go to college.

Serena was 14. Tennis fans and experts had awaited her debut. Her first tournament appearance was quick. She lost 6–1, 6–1 to American Annie Miller, ranked 149th in the world. But it was clear that Serena's power meant brighter days were ahead. Richard still did not want to rush Serena. She did not play another professional tournament for 17 months.

Serena returned to the Women's Tennis Association (WTA) circuit in 1997. She won six total matches in her first four

Venus, *left*, and Serena salute the crowd after their match at the 1998 Australian Open.

tournaments of the year. Then she made a splash in her fifth. It was the Ameritech Challenge. Serena beat Mary Pierce in the round of 16. Pierce was ranked seventh in the world. Then Serena beat fourth-ranked Monica Seles.

The next year, Serena competed in the Australian Open. It was her first Grand Slam event. She won her first match. But then she faced Venus. It was their first pro meeting. Venus showed that she had the edge on her sister. Serena kept it close in the first set. But Venus pulled away in the second.

Serena was starting to make waves in the tennis world. It would not be long before she climbed to the top of it.

Serena Williams

CHAPTER 3

UPS AND DOWNS

Serena Williams's rise to the top of the tennis world was as fast as one of her booming serves.

That loss to Venus Williams in the Australian Open was in January 1998. In September 1999, just 20 months later, Serena won the first of her many Grand Slam titles. That was when she beat Martina Hingis in the US Open final.

Serena's beads fly after a serve at a 1998 tournament.

Serena is known for her amazing serve. It is both powerful and accurate. She tosses the ball up the same way each time. That disguises where she is going to hit it. This leads to many aces.

In 1999 Serena broke into the top 10 of the WTA rankings. She finished the year ranked fourth. But that year was not only about tennis for Serena. She enrolled in the Art Institute of Fort Lauderdale. She wanted to study fashion design. It was the beginning of a big part of her life off the court.

Serena made just one Grand Slam final in the next two years. But she dominated in the two years after. Serena won the French Open, Wimbledon, and the US Open in 2002. Then she won the 2003 Australian Open. In each tournament, she beat Venus in the final.

Winning all four of those events in a calendar year is called a Grand Slam. But Serena did it differently. She won all four in

Serena celebrates with the championship trophy after winning her first Wimbledon singles title in 2002.

Serena has fun in practice before a 2002 tournament in Germany.

a row, just not in the same tennis season. Her achievement was called the "Serena Slam" or the "Sister Slam." The Wimbledon victory made her the top-ranked player in the world.

Serena was becoming very popular among fans. And it was not just because of her amazing play. Most fans considered tennis a traditional game. But Serena wasn't traditional. In August 2002, she played in a one-piece black outfit that looked like leather. It was very different from usual tennis attire. Writers and fans started taking note of her unique sense of style.

Serena won a second straight Wimbledon in 2003. But

> In September 2003, tragedy struck Serena's family. Her half sister Yetunde Price was killed in Los Angeles. She was shot about a mile from where Venus and Serena practiced tennis growing up.

disaster followed. A partially torn tendon in her knee required surgery. She thought she was only going to miss six or eight weeks. Then she expected to dominate again.

But she did not return for eight months. Serena took advantage of the time off. Besides fashion, she was also interested in acting. She appeared on TV shows and attended major sporting and pop culture events. She also worked on her own clothing line. She called it Aneres. That is Serena spelled backward. It launched in 2004.

Serena was not just a tennis star. She was a full-blown celebrity. Some critics thought she cared more about that than

Serena returns against Amelie Mauresmo in their semifinal match at Wimbledon in 2004.

she did about tennis. They doubted her ability to come back and win right away.

But Serena proved them wrong. She returned at the Nasdaq-100 Open in March 2004. And she took home the title.

She breezed through the final in less than an hour. Serena was flying high as she entered that year's Wimbledon final in July. But she lost to Maria Sharapova. Some called it one of the biggest upsets in Wimbledon history.

Things got worse in November. Serena met Sharapova again. This time it was in the final of the WTA Championships. Serena won the first set. But she pulled a stomach muscle in the second set. The pain was unbearable. She usually served 120 mph (193 km/h). But she could only manage about 70 mph (113 km/h) with the injury. Sharapova took advantage to win the title.

Serena had another up-and-down year in 2005. She won the Australian Open in January. It was her seventh Grand Slam singles title. But she had to miss the French Open in May due to an ankle injury. She finished the year ranked 11th in the world. It was the first time she had ended the year outside the top 10 since 1998.

The glory of the Serena Slam seemed so long ago.

Serena Williams

CHAPTER 4

COMING BACK STRONG

Players, fans, and sportswriters thought Williams cared more about off-court activities than tennis. She wanted to prove them wrong again. She started by winning the 2007 Australian Open. By the end of the year, she had climbed back to seventh in the world.

Williams continued climbing in 2008. She won three straight tournaments in March and April. She lost to Venus Williams in the Wimbledon final in June.

Williams, then ranked 81st in the world, celebrates her first-round win at the 2007 Australian Open.

But then she won the US Open in August. It was her ninth Grand Slam title. Serena completed her climb in 2009. She won the Australian Open and reclaimed her top ranking. Then she won Wimbledon.

She wanted to build off her 2009 success and stay healthy in 2010. She defended her Australian Open and Wimbledon titles. Serena was on a roll. Some were calling her one of the best tennis players ever. But then injury hit again.

In July she stepped on a piece of glass. The cuts to her foot were deep. She needed two surgeries. But things got worse. Treatment caused a blood clot in her lungs. She was rushed to the hospital in February 2011. The lung problems could have been fatal. But they were caught in time. Her career, though, was on hold.

Serena was named the Associated Press Female Athlete of the Year in 2009. It was her second time winning the award. She had also won in 2002. She went on to win it in 2013 and 2015, too.

Williams fought through injuries in 2011 but still made it to the US Open Final.

Williams finally returned to the court in June. Her ranking had fallen to 26th. She had missed three Grand Slam events. Once again she had a lot of work to do. She won tournaments in July and August. Then she lost the US Open final in September. It was the first time since 2006 she ended the season without a Grand Slam singles title. It would be a while before that happened again.

Serena's 2012 season started poorly. She lost in the first round of the French Open. She needed to make a change. So she started working with coach Patrick Mouratoglou.

The partnership led to greatness. In the following months, Serena won Wimbledon and the US Open. She also won the Olympic gold medal in women's singles. Adding that gave her a career Golden Slam.

In February 2013, Serena became the oldest top-ranked women's player. She was 31. She went on to win her 16th and 17th Grand Slam singles titles that year. Serena won 78 matches and 11 tournaments in 2013. Those were personal highs.

The 2012 French Open was a low point for Serena. She lost in the first round to Virginie Razzano. The French player was ranked 111th in the world. Through 2016 it was the only time Serena lost in the first round of a Grand Slam event.

But it got even better. Starting with the 2014 US Open and ending with 2015 Wimbledon, Serena won four straight majors. It was her second Serena Slam.

The 2015 Wimbledon win made her the oldest Grand Slam champion since the Open Era began in 1968. She was 33. It was a record she would soon break.

The Williams sisters hug after Serena, *right*, beat Venus for her record 23rd Grand Slam title at the 2017 Australian Open.

Serena won Wimbledon again in July 2016. Then in September, she tied Steffi Graf's record of 186 weeks in a row ranked number one. In January 2017, she won her 23rd Grand Slam title at the Australian Open. It was the most ever in the Open Era. To top it off, Serena revealed in April 2017 that she won the tournament while pregnant with her first child.

Serena proved that even at age 35, she was nearly impossible to beat. Her career began on cracked courts with no nets. And she will retire as one of the best of all time.

FUN FACTS AND QUOTES

- Serena and Venus Williams have dominated as doubles partners. They won their first 14 Grand Slam doubles finals matches from 1999 to 2016. They have each won Grand Slam doubles titles at least once. The Williams sisters have also won three Olympic gold medals in doubles.

- Serena has played Venus in nine Grand Slam singles finals. Serena has won seven of those matchups.

- Serena's competitiveness got her in trouble in 2009. She was serving in the US Open semifinal. It was match point for her opponent. An umpire called Serena for a foot fault. She had not faulted. Serena was livid. She threatened the umpire. She was penalized a point for the threat, which ended the match.

- The Williams sisters, who live in South Florida, are big football fans. In 2009 they bought a share of the Miami Dolphins.

- *"I prefer the (title), 'One of the greatest athletes of all time.'"* —Serena, when asked about being one of the greatest female athletes of all time

WEBSITES

To learn more about Playmakers, visit **abdobooklinks.com**. These links are routinely monitored and updated to provide the most current information available.

GLOSSARY

backhand
A tennis shot in which the player swings from the opposite side of his or her body from the hand holding the racket.

baseline
The line at each end of a tennis court.

clot
A collection of blood cells that stick together.

debut
A first appearance.

Grand Slam
One of the four most prestigious events in tennis; also refers to winning all four events in one year.

major
A Grand Slam event.

Open Era
An era beginning in 1968 when professional tennis players were allowed to play in Grand Slam tournaments with amateurs.

professional
An athlete who gets paid to play.

racism
Discrimination against other people based only on their race.

seed
A rank assigned to a player in a tournament.

tendon
A tough strand of tissue that connects muscle to bone.

INDEX

FURTHER RESOURCES

Kortemeier, Todd. *Greatest Female Athletes of All Time*. Minneapolis, MN: Abdo Publishing, 2017.

Shoup, Kate. *Serena Williams: International Tennis Superstar*. New York: Cavendish Square Publishing, 2016.

Uschan, Michael. *Serena Williams*. Detroit, MI: Lucent Books, 2011.